WALKS
ON THE
HOWGILL FELLS

HILLSIDE GUIDES

LONG DISTANCE WALKS
1 • THE WESTMORLAND WAY
2 • THE FURNESS WAY
3 • THE CUMBERLAND WAY
7 • CLEVELAND WAY COMPANION
9 • THE NORTH BOWLAND TRAVERSE
(by David Johnson)
16 • DALES WAY COMPANION
22 • THE COAST TO COAST WALK

CIRCULAR WALKS – YORKSHIRE DALES
4 • WALKS IN WHARFEDALE
5 • WALKS IN NIDDERDALE
6 • WALKS IN THE CRAVEN DALES
8 • WALKS IN WENSLEYDALE
10 • WALKS IN THREE PEAKS COUNTRY
11 • WALKS IN SWALEDALE
20 • RAMBLES IN WHARFEDALE
21 • WALKS ON THE HOWGILL FELLS

CIRCULAR WALKS – NORTH YORK MOORS
13 • WESTERN – Cleveland/Hambleton Hills
14 • SOUTHERN – Rosedale/Farndale/Bransdale
15 • NORTHERN – Eskdale and the Coast

CIRCULAR WALKS – SOUTH PENNINES
12 • WALKS IN BRONTE COUNTRY
17 • WALKS IN CALDERDALE

HILLWALKING – LAKE DISTRICT
18 • OVER LAKELAND MOUNTAINS
19 • OVER LAKELAND FELLS

FREEDOM OF THE DALES
40 selected walks
Full colour hardback

80 DALES WALKS
Omnibus edition of Books 4,6,8,11 and (in part)10,21
Published by Cordee, Leicester

WALKS
ON THE
HOWGILL FELLS

by

Paul Hannon

HILLSIDE PUBLICATIONS

HILLSIDE PUBLICATIONS
11 Nessfield Grove
Exley Head
Keighley
West Yorkshire
BD22 6NU

Page 1 illustration: Lune's Bridge
  (from Walk 6)

The maps in this book are based upon
the 1899-1920 Ordnance Survey 1:10,560 maps

ISBN   1 870141 14 8

Printed in Great Britain by
Carnmor Print and Design
95/97 London Road
Preston
Lancashire
PR1 4BA

INTRODUCTION

The Howgill Fells are a compact, well defined upland range, situated in the north-west corner of the Yorkshire Dales, yet wholly within Cumbria. Triangular in shape, the group is moated by the Lune on two sides and the Rawthey on the other. Across these rivers, however, is further unsung country that merits more than a passing glance, and so the scope of this guide is extended to include neighbours Uldale, Garsdale, Borrowdale and the Middleton and Frostrow Fells. The wooded riverbanks and colourful foothills are integral parts of the area, adding a greater diversity of scenery to the Howgills' special grandeur.

The hub of this otherwise sparsely populated district is Sedbergh, a smashing little town which is the largest community in the National Park. It sits regally at the foot of its fells, and presides over the convergence of the region's major roads and rivers. The supporting villages of Tebay and Ravenstonedale tidily occupy the other two corners of the Howgills' patch. A little further afield is the market town of Kirkby Stephen, while the nearest large town is Kendal, ten miles west of Sedbergh.

The fells are named from a settlement scattered along their western base — rather than the obvious choice of Sedbergh — and even this only found its way onto maps in quite recent times. This alone may have helped keep the hills relatively undisturbed: certainly more people gasp at their splendour from 70mph on the motorway than ever set foot on their inviting slopes.

The terrain of the Howgill Fells is such that it encourages long strides over its grassy ridges, a lack of internal walls instilling a sense of freedom not sensed elsewhere in the Dales. Rarely in evidence is the underlying slate, though when revealed it is done in some style, at the remarkable ravines of Cautley and Carlingill. This walkers' paradise is a no-man's-land where Dales and Lakes meet, the characteristics of both being present without either dominating. This identity crisis is fuelled by the fact that only half of the main group is within the National Park, for the northern dales and ridges of old Westmorland are accorded no such status.

In spite of its isolation the area is ringed by main roads, and is made further accessible by the Settle-Carlisle Railway: stations at Garsdale Head and Kirkby Stephen make it a most practical as well as scenically magnificent line.

SOME USEFUL FACILITIES

There are youth hostels at Tebay and Kirkby Stephen

	Accommodation	Inn	Car park	Bus service	Post office	other shop	Payphone	WC
Barbon	•	•	•			•	•	
Cautley	•	unlicensed						
Garsdale Foot	•		•	•				
Garsdale Head	•	•	•				•	
Howgill	•						•	
Lowgill	•						•	
Middleton	•	•		•				
Millthrop			•				•	
Ravenstonedale	•	•	•					
Sedbergh	•	•	•	•	•	•	•	•
Tebay	•	•		•	•	•		•

ORDNANCE SURVEY MAPS

Although the strip-maps illustrating each walk are sufficient to guide one safely around, they cannot depict the surrounding countryside, nor show the adjoining paths should one wish to amend any particular route. An Ordnance Survey map will thus make an ideal companion.

1:50,000 Landranger sheets 91, 97, 98

1:25,000
Pathfinder 607 (NY 60/70) - Walks 3, 6, 8, 11, 15
617 (SD 69/79) - Walks 1, 4, 5, 7, 8, 9, 10, 13-16
628 (SD 67/68) - Walk 12
Outdoor Leisure 2 Yorkshire Dales West - Walks 2, 14
7 English Lakes SE - Walk 6

SOME USEFUL ADDRESSES

Ramblers' Association
1/5 Wandsworth Road, London SW8 2XX
Tel. 071- 582 6878

Youth Hostels Association
Trevelyan House, St. Albans, Herts. AL1 2DY
Tel. 0727 - 55215

Yorkshire Dales National Park Office
Colvend, Hebden Road, Grassington, Skipton BD23 5LB
Tel. 0756 - 752748

Sedbergh National Park Centre
Main Street, Sedbergh, LA10 5AD
Tel. 05396 - 20125

Kirkby Stephen Tourist Information
Market Street, Kirkby Stephen CA17 4QN
Tel. 07683 - 71199

Yorkshire Dales Society
Otley Civic Centre, Cross Green, Otley LS21 1HD
Tel. 0943 - 607868

British Rail
Leeds -   0532- 448133
Carlisle -   0228- 44711

Bus operators

Cumberland Motor Services, Kendal   Tel. 0539 - 733221

Details of all services, including local operators:
Cumbrian Connections, Cumbria County Council, Carlisle
Tel. 0228 - 812812

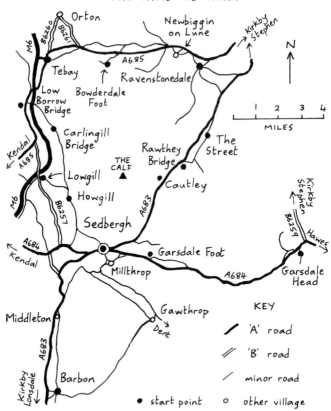

The 16 walks described range in length from 3¾ to 12½ miles, and the terrain similarly varies from riverside strolls to rather more strenuous moorland outings. All walks are circular, and with an average distance of 6½ miles are ideally suited to half-day rambles. Each walk is given its own chapter consisting of 'immediate impression' diagram, detailed narrative and strip-map and notes and illustrations of features of interest along the way.

KEY TO THE MAP SYMBOLS

Route — clear — sketchy — no path

Route on public road — unenclosed — wall — Fence/hedge

Abbreviations g = gate
s = stile c = cattle grid

Railway line

Buildings   Church   Cairns
summit other   Limestone clints

Crags   Loose rock/scree   Marsh   Trees

river or beck   tarn or lake
bridge   waterfall

Miles from start   Direction of North   N
③

Scale: approximately 2½ inches = 1 mile

THE COUNTRY CODE

- Respect the life and work of the countryside
- Protect wildlife, plants and trees
- Keep to public paths across farmland
- Safeguard water supplies
- Go carefully on country roads
- Keep dogs under control
- Guard against all risks of fire
- Fasten all gates
- Leave no litter - take it with you
- Make no unnecessary noise
- Leave livestock, crops and machinery alone
- Use gates and stiles to cross fences, hedges and walls

THE WALKS

Listed below are the 16 walks
described, the walk number being the
key to easy location in the guide

WALK	TITLE	MILES
1	THE ASCENT OF THE CALF	$6\frac{1}{4}$
2	FROSTROW FELLS AND MILLTHROP	$6\frac{3}{4}$
3	THE ASCENT OF GREEN BELL	$6\frac{3}{4}$
4	THE GRISEDALE LANDSCAPE	$3\frac{3}{4}$
5	CARLINGILL AND BLACK FORCE	$4\frac{1}{2}$
6	BORROWDALE AND THE LUNE GORGE	$7\frac{1}{4}$
7	THE DOWBIGGIN AREA	$6\frac{1}{2}$
8	BOWDERDALE AND HAZELGILL KNOTT	$8\frac{1}{4}$
9	FOX'S PULPIT AND THE LUNE	$7\frac{1}{2}$
10	THE ULDALE WATERFALLS	$5\frac{3}{4}$
11	BLEASE FELL AND TEBAY GILL	6
12	THE MIDDLETON FELL CIRCUIT	$12\frac{1}{2}$
13	ARANT HAW, WINDER AND CROOK	$5\frac{1}{2}$
14	LOWER GARSDALE	$6\frac{1}{4}$
15	STENNERSKEUGH AND FELL END CLOUDS	$3\frac{3}{4}$
16	CAUTLEY SPOUT AND THE RAWTHEY	$6\frac{1}{4}$

THE WALKS

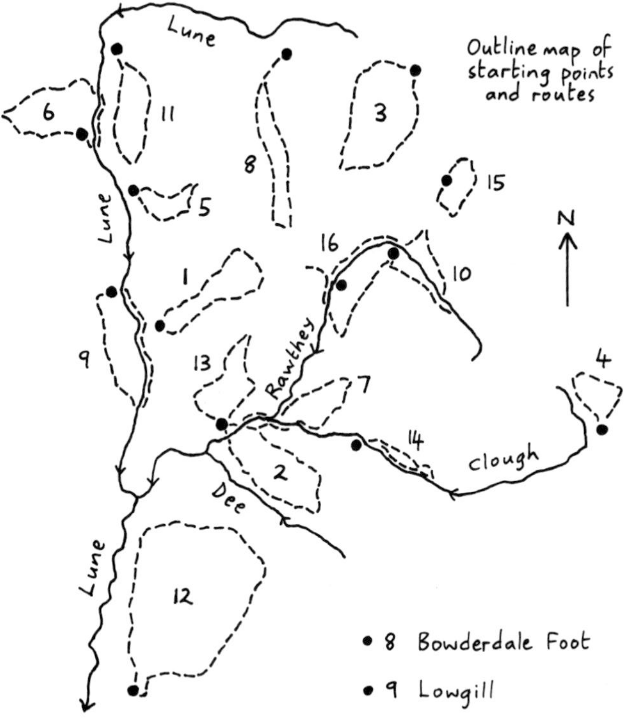

Outline map of starting points and routes

N ↑

- 1 Howgill
- 2 Sedbergh
- 3 Ravenstonedale
- 4 Garsdale Head
- 5 Carlingill Bridge
- 6 Low Borrow Bridge
- 7 Sedbergh
- 8 Bowderdale Foot
- 9 Lowgill
- 10 Rawthey Bridge
- 11 Tebay
- 12 Barbon
- 13 Sedbergh
- 14 Garsdale Foot
- 15 The Street
- 16 Cautley

WALK 1

6¼ miles

THE ASCENT OF THE CALF

From Howgill

Outstanding green pathways on archetypal Howgill ridges present a magnificent circuit over the crown of the Howgill Fells

looking north-east

Howgill church is 2¾ miles along Howgill Lane out of Sedbergh, sat in a hollow behind a gated road. There is room for thoughtful parking alongside. A modest donation in the collecting box inside this lovely church would be a nice gesture for the use of the verge. Squeezing vehicles into the passing places and verges of Howgill Lane is likely to obstruct local traffic.

THE WALK

Back on Howgill Lane, turn left over the bridge (away from Sedbergh) and up the hill to the farm of Gate Side, where a stile on the right is the start of a field-path rising to Castley, short-cutting the road junction at Four Lane Ends. It crosses to a gate, over a beck, straight up to a stile on the brow. Going right with the fence, take a gate in the wall that takes over and head up through the pasture to Castley. Spiral up between the farm buildings and turn right along the enclosed track to a gate onto the open fell.

The broad track curves beneath Castley Knotts and down to a ford over Long Rigg Beck. Immediately across, a green track commences an assault on the grassy rib of White Fell, initially steeply through bracken, then gently up the long spur. When the going eases on White Fell

Head, the path curves round to the right to omit the minor summit, and absorbs another path for the short, final pull up to the top of the Calf, with its waiting Ordnance column.

Leave by the broad 'tourist' path heading south for Sedbergh, but in the first depression fork to the right, slanting across the upper dome of Bram Rigg Top on a super path. Descending the distinct ridge, the way passes through a series of rock cuttings and past a sheepfold to a fork on the now level ridge. Branch left to drop down to ford Bram Rigg Beck, across which the track initially scales the flank opposite before traversing under Seat Knott to arrive at the intake wall. A little further along to the left a gate leads off the fell, and a pleasant farm track runs down to Birkhaw.

Turning through a gate alongside the farmhouse, an invisible field-path descends by Smithy Beck to meet the road just south of the church.

The setting of Castley Farm is entirely enviable, with the Calf and its entourage watching over. Of the similarly appointed tops, it is the Calf itself that, surprisingly, appears of least significance.

The homely church of the Holy Trinity is the heart of Howgill's scattered farming community.

Castley (Farm)

CARLINGILL ↑

CROOK OF LUNE BRIDGE ←

Four Lane Ends

Chapel Beck

Gate Side (Farm)

Howgill

Smithy Beck

⑥

Birkhaw (Farm)

SEDBERGH

Fell Head from White Fell Head ↓

The hoary cairn illustrated merits a detour for the view it reveals of, a mile north, the 'Horse of Busha' on Bush Howe. It is also a rare and useful shelter.

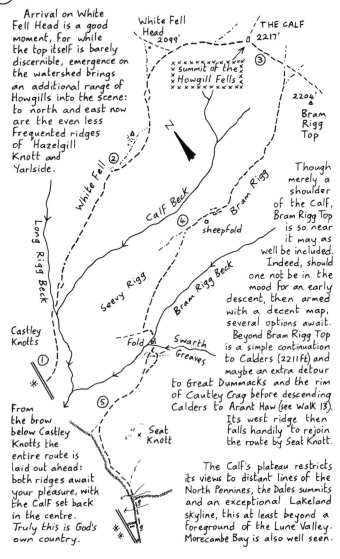

Arrival on White Fell Head is a good moment, for while the top itself is barely discernible, emergence on the watershed brings an additional range of Howgills into the scene: to north and east now are the even less frequented ridges of Hazelgill Knott and Yarlside.

White Fell Head 2099'

THE CALF 2217'

× × × × × × × × × ×
× summit of the ×
× Howgill Fells ×
× × × × × × × × × × ×

③

2204' Bram Rigg Top

White Fell ②

Long Rigg Beck

Calf Beck

Bram Rigg

④

sheepfold

Seevy Rigg

Bram Rigg Beck

Castley Knotts

①

✳

Fold

Swarth Greaves

⑤

Seat Knott

Though merely a shoulder of the Calf, Bram Rigg Top is so near it may as well be included. Indeed, should one not be in the mood for an early descent, then armed with a decent map, several options await.

Beyond Bram Rigg Top is a simple continuation to Calders (2211ft) and maybe an extra detour to Great Dummacks and the rim of Cautley Crag before descending Calders to Arant Haw (see Walk 13). Its west ridge then falls handily to rejoin the route by Seat Knott.

From the brow below Castley Knotts the entire route is laid out ahead: both ridges await your pleasure, with the Calf set back in the centre. Truly this is God's own country.

✳

✳

The Calf's plateau restricts its views to distant lines of the North Pennines, the Dales summits and an exceptional Lakeland skyline, this at least beyond a foreground of the Lune Valley. Morecambe Bay is also well seen.

WALK 2

FROSTROW FELLS AND MILLTHROP

6¾ miles

from Sedbergh

Splendid mountain scenery from
the feet of two valleys

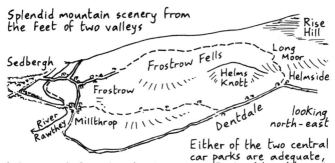

Either of the two central
car parks are adequate,
but a start from the lay-by at New Bridge (where the road
to Hawes crosses the Rawthey) is more satisfactory.

THE WALK

New Bridge is reached by heading east along the
main street and branching right on the Hawes road at the
edge of town. After crossing the bridge remain on the main
road only as far as the first junction, and heading along
the narrow lane ignore branches left and then right to
continue along the 'no through road' that is Frostrow Lane.
It leads past several farms to an eventual demise alongside
High Side Farm, and a stile directly ahead empties onto
the Frostrow Fells.

Follow the track heading away along a minor ridge,
with the dome of Rise Hill as a guide. Beyond a nearby
wall-corner and barn, a wall-corner is reached above Holebeck
Gill. The improved way rises as a sunken track above the beck,
and as it peters out a slim trod takes up the running to
slant up to the wall marking the watershed.

Head left with the wall as far as a stile, and take
the green, wallside track bound for Dentdale. This is vacated,
however, at the first stile in it, to now shadow another wall
heading away. Through a gate the way steepens towards the
valley bottom, a track forming to lead through a gate at
the bottom left of this large enclosure. Continuing down
to Helmside, use a gate on the right to pass by the farm and
emerge onto the road alongside Dent Crafts Centre.

15

Turn right along the valley road for three-quarters of a mile, to leave it at the second cluster of buildings: Craggs Farm is readily identifiable as it is entirely on the left side of the road. Take the gate opposite and head up to a stile in the adjacent wall, then slant up to Leakses. Passing in front of the farmhouse go left to a gate by the farthest barn, then crossing several fields and rising slightly to Burton Hill Farm. Pass between the buildings and up to an ornate gate, then cross a field-bottom before aiming for Hewthwaite, the next farm. From a stile by the nearest barn, cross to a stile below a gate opposite, to cross two further fields to emerge onto the drive to Gap Farm by way of a near-hidden stile.

Pass along the front of the house, over a field and along the foot of Gap Wood. Enclosed for much of the way, a superb green track leaves the trees behind to round the ridge-end towards Sedbergh. At a distinct fork keep right to a stile, joining a wide track that winds down through the golf course and becomes enclosed to enter Millthrop. Go right to a junction and left to Millthrop Bridge to re-enter Sedbergh. For New Bridge, simply take the riverside path instead: a grand finish.

see also page 31

GARSDALE A684

Former pinfold

Frostrow

Frostrow Lane

Side Farm

①

Frostrow is a widely scattered farming community, devoid of a nucleus. A small Methodist chapel stands on the main road a little further east. Frostrow's straggling lane serves up a fine prospect of the Howgills, which broadens on gaining the open fell.

New Bridge

R. Rawthey

Sedbergh

ROAD

⑥

DENT

Millthrop

club house

golf course

Gap Wood

Millthrop is a tightly packed community incorporating a terrace of mill cottages and a curiously shaped Methodist chapel.

Arrival above the golf course is a breathtaking moment. In front are the Howgill Fells majestically dominating Sedbergh, with the Lune Valley to the west: perfect in evening sunlight.

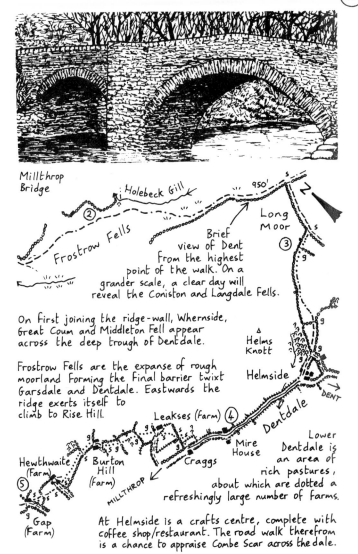

Millthrop Bridge

Holebeck Gill

②

950'

Long Moor

Frostrow Fells

③

Brief view of Dent from the highest point of the walk. On a grander scale, a clear day will reveal the Coniston and Langdale Fells.

On first joining the ridge-wall, Whernside, Great Coum and Middleton Fell appear across the deep trough of Dentdale.

△ Helms Knott

Helmside

DENT

Frostrow Fells are the expanse of rough moorland forming the final barrier twixt Garsdale and Dentdale. Eastwards the ridge exerts itself to climb to Rise Hill.

Leakses (Farm) ④

Dentdale

Mire House

Craggs

Lower Dentdale is an area of rich pastures, about which are dotted a refreshingly large number of farms.

Hewthwaite (Farm)

Burton Hill (Farm)

MILLTHROP

⑤

Gap (Farm)

At Helmside is a crafts centre, complete with coffee shop/restaurant. The road walk therefrom is a chance to appraise Combe Scar across the dale.

17

WALK 3

6¾ miles

THE ASCENT OF GREEN BELL

from Ravenstonedale

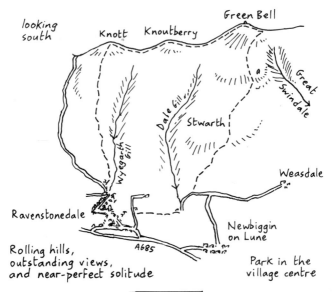

looking south

Rolling hills, outstanding views, and near-perfect solitude

Park in the village centre

THE WALK

From the junction outside the school turn down to the bridge by the church, left to the King's Head and out along the road to the by-pass. Before the main road is reached, turn left up a 'no through road' to Greenside. It is left at the first gate on the right, following the wall away to enter an enclosed green lane. When it prematurely expires maintain the same line through the fields to drop down past a barn and emerge via a drive onto a road-end at The Hollow.

Go left with the road up towards a brow, but as a tractor track branches left, follow it onto the broad northern flanks of Green Bell. Avoiding the dampness of Tailor Mire, it makes a cautious start on the slope ahead. Occasionally sketchy, it slants ever half-right up past a fenced enclosure and soon improves as it rises to a well

18

defined corner above a walled enclosure. Rounding the bend it forks, and here take the upper branch curving onto the shoulder of Stwarth.

With the stones of Hunthoof Pike prominent ahead, a clear grass track climbs steadily up the better defined ridge. The 'pike' is found to require a detour, the track itself rising ever more clearly to slant across Green Bell's upper cone to a saddle south-west of the top. This is a supreme moment, and from here a clear path doubles back up to the left to the waiting Ordnance column.

The summit is vacated by a thin path heading east, almost at once dropping steeply to a sheepfold. Already in view is Ravenstonedale, and the finest way back utilises thin trods continuing east over the minor tops (both cairned) of Knoutberry and Knott. Striking north off the latter, a previously encountered path is joined above an island field. From the foot of this enclosure a super green track heads unerringly down the fell, emerging onto an access road to arrive at Town Head.

An interesting finish avoids the road by crossing to a brace of wooden bridges on the left, thence dropping down through the 'back' of the village.

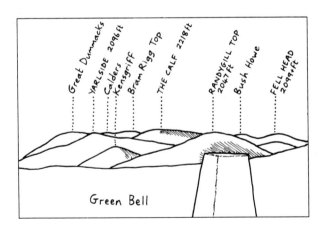

The Howgill Fells from Green Bell's summit

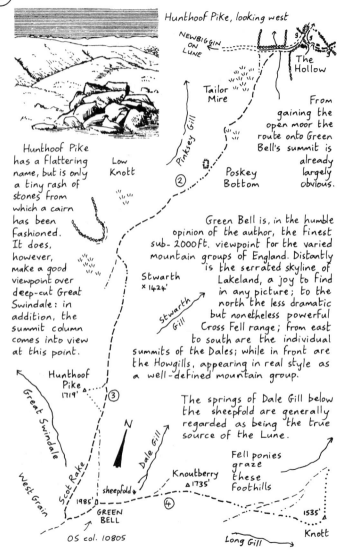

Hunthoof Pike, looking west

NEWBIGGIN ON LUNE

The Hollow

Tailor Mire

Pinksey Gill

Low Knott

②

Poskey Bottom

From gaining the open moor the route onto Green Bell's summit is already largely obvious.

Hunthoof Pike has a flattering name, but is only a tiny rash of stones from which a cairn has been fashioned. It does, however, make a good viewpoint over deep-cut Great Swindale: in addition, the summit column comes into view at this point.

Green Bell is, in the humble opinion of the author, the finest sub-2000 ft. viewpoint for the varied mountain groups of England. Distantly is the serrated skyline of Lakeland, a joy to find in any picture; to the north the less dramatic but nonetheless powerful Cross Fell range; from east to south are the individual summits of the Dales; while in front are the Howgills, appearing in real style as a well-defined mountain group.

Stwarth × 1424'

Stwarth Gill

Hunthoof Pike 1719'
③

Great Swindale

West Grain

Scot Rake

1985'

GREEN BELL

OS col. 1080.5

N

Dale Gill

sheepfold

Knoutberry △ 1735'

④

The springs of Dale Gill below the sheepfold are generally regarded as being the true source of the Lune.

Fell ponies graze these foothills

1535' △
Knott

Long Gill

20

Ravenstonedale is one of the loveliest of old Westmorland villages, nestling at the foot of the Howgill Fells but also set below a limestone landscape spread to the north. A homely cluster of dwellings repose respectfully back from the attractive church. Dating from the mid-eighteenth century, it overlooks the site of a 12th century cell of the Gilbertine canons. Two hostelries, pleasant beck scenery, some charming cottages - look out for a surviving spinning gallery - add to the delights of this village known locally as 'Rassendl'.

These innocuous pastures mark the important Lune/Eden watershed, the major North-South Cumbrian divide, with one river bound for Carlisle, the other Lancaster.

TEBAY

① ruin

Low Greenside

Lockholme Beck

Ravenstonedale

✴ inns

A685

by pass

A685

KIRKBY STEPHEN

Scandal Beck

TO A683

Kilmire

TO A683

ADAMTHWAITE

N

⑥

Wyegarth Gill

⑤

St. Oswalds Ravenstonedale

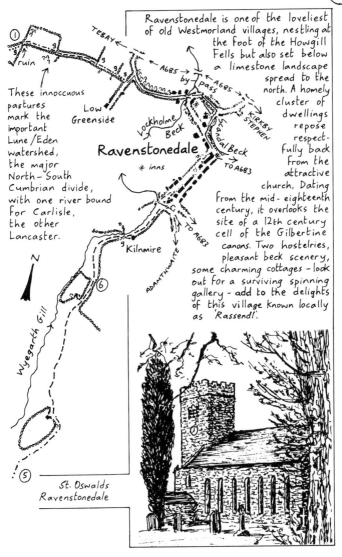

WALK 4
3¾ miles

THE GRISEDALE LANDSCAPE
from Garsdale Head

An unglamorous stroll through a bleak Dales upland - great!

looking north-east

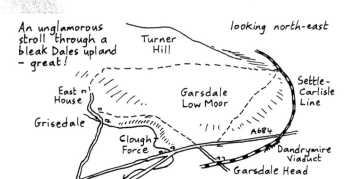

Turner Hill

East House

Grisedale

Garsdale Low Moor

Settle-Carlisle Line

Clough Force

A684

Dandrymire Viaduct

Garsdale Head

Park on the road climbing from the main road to the railway station

THE WALK

Descend to the main road and cross straight over to a stile. Head straight up the pasture to the next stile, from where the waterfall of Clough Force can be espied by a detour to the left. Back on top, maintain a direct line for Grisedale, guided by a prominent tree towards the farm buildings of Blake Mire. From a stile to the right, a series of stiles slant down to the valley. Without immediately joining the road, take a stile by some barns to remain parallel with it, only meeting it at Moor Rigg beyond a further stile.

Turn right along the now unenclosed road as far as its demise at East House, then continue up the track onto the open moor. Fork right by the intake wall, and as the way fades curve steadily left on a level course to see both stile and gate in the wall ahead. Beyond, descend rough pasture to a footbridge over the railway. Do not cross it, but squeeze between the line and the house, and head diagonally away to a collapsed wall. Rising behind, use a depression between two gentle slopes to locate a stile. Now a sketchy trod picks a way across two further pastures before a direct descent to the main road, emerging opposite a farm.

The road junction is now two minutes to the right.

Swarth Fell from Blake Mire

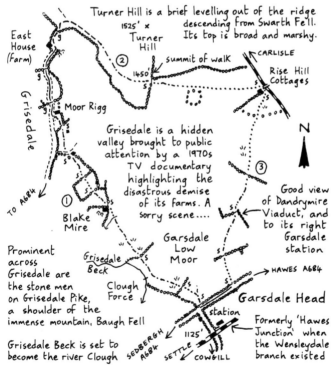

Turner Hill is a brief levelling out of the ridge descending from Swarth Fell. Its top is broad and marshy.

East House (Farm)

1525' x Turner Hill

② 1450'

summit of walk

CARLISLE

Rise Hill Cottages

Grisedale

Moor Rigg

Grisedale is a hidden valley brought to public attention by a 1970s TV documentary highlighting the disastrous demise of its farms. A sorry scene....

N

③

Good view of Dandrymire Viaduct, and to its right Garsdale station

TO A684

① Blake Mire

Grisedale Beck

Garsdale Low Moor

HAWES A684

Prominent across Grisedale are the stone men on Grisedale Pike, a shoulder of the immense mountain, Baugh Fell

Clough Force ↓

Garsdale Head

station

Formerly 'Hawes Junction' when the Wensleydale branch existed

Grisedale Beck is set to become the river Clough

SEDBERGH A684

1125'

SETTLE

COWGILL

23

WALK 5

4½ miles

from Carlingill Bridge

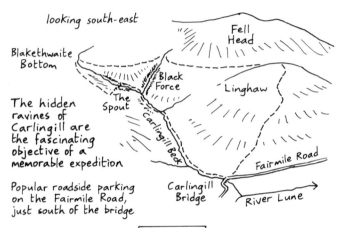

looking south-east

Fell Head

Blakethwaite Bottom

Black Force

The Spout

Linghaw

The hidden ravines of Carlingill are the fascinating objective of a memorable expedition

Carlingill Beck

Fairmile Road

Popular roadside parking on the Fairmile Road, just south of the bridge

Carlingill Bridge

River Lune

THE WALK

From Carlingill Bridge turn to follow the beck up its enclosed course, a clear path materialising to remain largely evident all the way. The hills increasingly close in, and at the second inflowing gill on the right, the valley narrows markedly. Though there appears no obvious means of progress, cross to the opposite bank: a rough wall of scree tumbles to the deeply carved gill, but after a brief pull a surprise path is found to traverse cautiously across. Its return to the floor of the gill coincides with the spectacular moment of arrival at the foot of the ravine of Black Force.

The confluence here is a situation to savour, and indeed to take stock of the next stage. Two options await, and if that last section has given enough excitement then a direct route crosses the left-hand (main) beck to commence a steep pull up the inviting rib on the left side of Black Force's ravine. If bound for further thrills and spills, keep faith with the floor of Carlin Gill. Initially there seems to be no obvious way again, but a trodden path soon forms to clamber its way along the right-hand (south) bank. Passing a lovely waterslide this absorbing path is halted all too soon at the

24

impasse of the Spout, a stunning waterfall that will not be fully seen until penetrating to the limit of exploration.

Escape comes by crossing the beek to a choice of a steep, stony pull or a cleaner scramble up the tilted rock: either demands caution, while the latter earns an even more intimate view of the Spout. On the flank above, continue up steep grass to a level trod that lends itself to a stroll along to the hollow of Blakethwaite Bottom. Cross the thin branch of the beek to a clearer path opposite, there doubling back to cross the main arm of the beek. Now take the upper of two slender ways heading off across the grass, rising just a little before aiming for the unmistakable head of Black Force.

The mercurial path returns high above the gorge of upper Carlin Gill to arrive at the calm upper reaches above Black Force. Across the stream the main path makes a short climb, while a lower alternative slants more gently across to the rough terrain at the head of the ravine, a most dramatic vantage point. Back on the upper path, it rounds this north shoulder of Fell Head and sets forth on a wonderful traverse around to a col linking the minor top of Linghaw with its parent fell.

At this neat crossroads of green ways turn right to surmount the grassy brow of Linghaw and then slope gently down to a useful trod. With the Lune Gorge outspread below the finish is an obvious one, tracing the long shoulder of the fell back down to the start. Though sketchy in places, the breaks in the path can be easily linked up, though in practise this is of little consequence.

The Spout

The Spout and Black Force are two remarkable physical features secreted in the folds of Carlin Gill. Each has been named well, for the former pours as if from a major leak into its colourful amphitheatre, while Black Force is a series of tumbling little falls throughout the full length of a dark-walled ravine.

The elevated return leg is along the upper flanks of Fell Head, one of the Howgills' four 2000 foot mountains. Grand views are on permanent offer, from the high peaks of central Lakeland to the waters of Morecambe Bay.

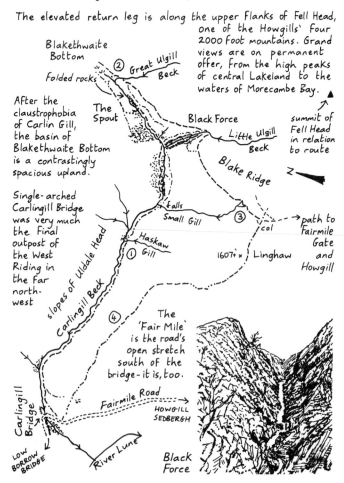

Blakethwaite Bottom

② Great Ulgill Beck

Folded rocks

The Spout

Black Force

Little Ulgill Beck

Blake Ridge

summit of Fell Head in relation to route

N

After the claustrophobia of Carlin Gill, the basin of Blakethwaite Bottom is a contrastingly spacious upland.

Single-arched Carlingill Bridge was very much the final outpost of the West Riding in the far north-west

falls

Small Gill

③

col

→ path to Fairmile Gate and Howgill

slopes of Uldale Head

① Haskaw Gill

1607' x Linghaw

Carlingill Beck

④

The 'Fair Mile' is the road's open stretch south of the bridge - it is, too.

Carlingill Bridge

Fairmile Road →

HOWGILL SEDBERGH

LOW BORROW BRIDGE

River Lune

Black Force

WALK 6

| BORROWDALE AND THE LUNE GORGE |

7¼ miles   from Low Borrow Bridge

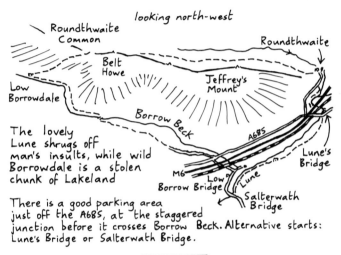

looking north-west

Roundthwaite Common

Belt Howe

Low Borrowdale

Jeffrey's Mount

Roundthwaite

Borrow Beck

A685

Lune's Bridge

M6   Low Borrow Bridge

Lune

Salterwath Bridge

The lovely Lune shrugs off man's insults, while wild Borrowdale is a stolen chunk of Lakeland

There is a good parking area just off the A685, at the staggered junction before it crosses Borrow Beck. Alternative starts: Lune's Bridge or Salterwath Bridge.

| THE WALK |

From the parking area a gentle start leads into the heart of Borrowdale, heading through the gate and following the initially surfaced farm road up the valley. The ensuing rough road crosses Borrow Beck and runs along to the farm of Low Borrowdale. Take the gate to the left of the house and at once forsake the valley track by doubling back up one to the right. It climbs above the farm and through a couple of fields onto the open fell.

On the very verge of the ridge-top the way suddenly expires: head straight on through the grassy saddle and drop down to the marshy beginnings of a beck. Keeping left of it, a sketchy way drops down again to meet a track coming in from the left. This swings round, parallel with the beck down to the right, to falter on wet ground before re-appearing at a patch of bracken to wind down to cross the beck. All is now clear as a broad track heads away, being joined by a wall and eventually descending to Roundthwaite.

A green track swings right to meet the narrow road,

turning right for just a few yards before dropping down to pick up a thin path by Roundthwaite Beck. This is shadowed through its final yards to a confluence with the Lune, just prior to the motorway bridge. Unclear on the ground, the right of way climbs back to the road to cross motorway, railway and river by the elevated A685, while directly ahead an inviting anglers' path accompanies the Lune under the bridges and rises from a stile to the road-end at Lune's Bridge. Just above Lune's Bridge is the modern A685, which must be crossed to head off down-river on the farm road to Brockholes.

Running high above the Lune, the way eventually halts at the isolated farm, whereupon turn immediately down to gain the bank of the Lune behind the buildings. It is now simply a case of strolling by the river, to conclude with a woodland path onto the road at Salterwath Bridge. Turn right over the bridge, rising past the farm and Roman Fort at Low Borrow Bridge before a final encounter with railway and motorway brings us back to the A685, almost opposite the start.

Roundthwaite Common

1427' x

1122' x Birk Knott

Burn Gill

N

Low Borrowdale (farm)

(3)

x Belt Howe 1338'

(2) 1C

Borrow Beck

(1)

The short but enjoyable climb above the farm earns a glorious retrospective view over Borrowdale, to the rangy heights of Grayrigg Common and Whinfell Beacon opposite.

Low Borrowdale sits in happy seclusion, the only farm in the six miles of the valley between the A6 and the dale's demise at Low Borrow Bridge. Appropriately enough it has the look of a Lakeland farmstead, for the valley itself, locked in a no-man's-land between Dales and Lakes, exhibits a greater affinity with the eastern valleys of the latter. Indeed, Borrowdale starts out within the Lakes' boundary – though Lakeland tourists know only one Borrowdale! It was, however, sufficiently beautiful to attract the covetous eyes of the water board not so long ago – they didn't get it though.

With road, railway and latterly motorway joining the river Lune in its squeeze through the gorge, this is an animated scene in the midst of an otherwise remote location. It was the stealthy northward encroachment of the M6 in 1970 that brought greatest upheaval, the end result being that both Low Borrow and Lune's Bridges were made virtually redundant, the latter entirely so. The endless whine of traffic cannot ruin this fair scene, however, for the stranded bridge strides as always over the Lune as it funnels through a narrow ravine. The grassy terrace atop the gorge makes a suitable spot for a sojourn.

Unmistakable at Low Borrow Bridge is the elevated mound of a Roman Fort.

Roundthwaite – a farming hamlet

Roundthwaite Beck

Lune's Bridge

Casterfell Hill and Jeffrey's Mount suggest an obvious and easy high-level alternative route to Roundthwaite

Casterfell Hill
× 1204'

1240' × Jeffrey's Mount

Semi-wild ponies graze Roundthwaite Common, while the very fortunate might glimpse a 'Haweswater' eagle wheeling high over Borrowdale.

River Lune

N

Borrow Beck

Brockholes (Farm)

L = Low Borrow Bridge

R = Roman Fort

Borrowdale Wood

START

Borrowdale Wood contains a fine deciduous mixture.

Borrow Beck's confluence with the Lune is well seen from near Brockholes.

Salterwath Bridge is a local rarity – it still retains its usefulness!

The old main road comes in between these farm buildings

Salterwath Bridge

CARLINGILL

29

WALK 7

6½ miles

from Sedbergh

A fascinating perambulation by two rivers and two gills: enchanting scenery

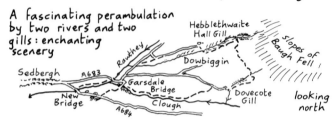

There are two car parks in the centre of Sedbergh, though the lay-by at New Bridge is actually most handily placed

THE WALK

From the main street head east, to branch right on the Hawes road at the edge of town. Soon after crossing New Bridge the road narrows, and care is needed until the first junction on the left brings relief. A rough lane runs down to Garsdale Bridge, which is crossed to take a stile and shadow the Clough upstream. Above a wooded bank the path descends to the river, and now adheres to its winding course until just past a footbridge. Here we are deflected up by another wooded bank.

This time there is no return to the river, for the sketchy path that has materialised maintains its rise over the pastures, on a generally obvious line to a stile before a marshy enclosure. Bearing left here, a clearer track forms and skirts round to the left. At the end it swings left to a gate, and here go right to the next gate where a short-lived stony, enclosed way climbs to Dowbiggin Lane. Turn right along its narrow course, and keep straight on along the short drive to Dovecote Gill.

Passing between the farm buildings, take a gate on the right to drop down to the wooded environs of the gill itself. Across a simple footbridge a path goes left to climb to a stile, leaving the gill as quickly as we entered it. A winding green track climbs the pasture above to a gate onto the open fell at a collapsed limekiln. Turn left along a track above the intake wall, crossing Dovecote Gill at the head of its secret ravine ●*CONTINUED ON PAGE 32, OVERLEAF*●

30

Sedbergh is the largest community in the Yorkshire Dales National Park, yet its isolation has helped it avoid the excesses of commercialism. Ceded to Cumbria in 1974, Sedbergh – omit the last two letters in pronunciation – was previously in the north-western extremity of the West Riding of Yorkshire, incredibly over 100 miles distant from its West Riding colleague Sheffield. Two simple facts illustrating size is very much a relative thing.

This tiny market town boasts an unparalleled position on the lower slopes of its 'own' mountains the Howgill Fells, and the outlook on three sides is, in fact, of fells. This is the edge of the Dales, and to the west of the town runs the river Lune. In the neighbourhood of Sedbergh three lively rivers end their journeys, as the Dee, Clough and Rawthey join forces to swell the waters of the Lune.

Aside from the imposing Howgill Fells, Sedbergh itself is dominated by its public school. This famous establishment, which was founded in the early 16th century, includes Adam Sedgwick the geologist among its old boys. The oldest remaining part dates from 1716, and is now the library. Most other features of interest will be found on or near the lengthy main street, including a lovely parish church in an equally attractive wooded surround. Dedicated to St. Andrew it has a 15th century tower, with other parts dating back to Norman times as well as many other periods in between.

St. Andrew's
Sedbergh

before continuing along the base of Baugh Fell.

A spell away from the wall sees us near it again at Fellgate Farm, to then cut another corner to run by an old limekiln. On the brow behind – as the track forsakes the wall once more – a supreme moment awaits, with the wooded course of Hebblethwaite Hall Gill backed by an uninterrupted Howgills panorama. It is easiest now to work back down to the wall as it approaches the gill, passing by shakeholes to arrive at a gate that will take us off the Fell. Before that, however, the highlight of the walk beckons, in the scarred wall of the twisted ravine just ahead. Its wonders can be ideally sampled by stepping out along the projecting rib immediately in front – truly a place to linger!

On resuming, go through the gate and make use of the parapet heading away. As the thin green way fades, press on along the brow of the pasture, with our objective of Hebblethwaite Hall high across the gill. Beyond a gateway the path drops left to trail around the perimeter of the pasture, though the immediate goal is a pair of gateposts down to the right. From them plunge straight down into the trees. A path descends steeply to a footbridge, and a similar re-ascent leads to a field-crossing to arrive at the entrance to Hebblethwaite Hall.

Go left along its drive, and when it eventually goes sharp right, take a gate on the left to maintain a straight line along the hedge to approach Ghyllas. On joining the drive, go just yards to the right to locate a path along the side of a garage, running briefly through trees to descend to the A683. Accommodating verges lead down to cross the Rawthey at Straight Bridge, across which a stile begins the final leg, a simple, attractive riverside stroll.

At once there is added interest as the Clough pours in for a major confluence, ending its days with a flourish in the form of a low waterfall. Doubled in power, the Rawthey now returns us to New Bridge.

The mill at Garsdale Bridge is very large for the locality, and is still put to use, at least in part.

This is a lovely spot, with the Dent Fault ensuring superior river scenery.

The ravine,
Hebblethwaite
Hall Gill,
looking
to the
Howgill Fells

The ravine of Hebblethwaite Hall Gill is superbly sited where the gill vacates the bare moor for the rich woodland. This is a stunning locale in the Dent Fault country, the gorge carved through walls of slabby rock.

Hebblethwaite Hall Woods are in the capable hands of the Woodland Trust — visitors welcome

The farms of Dowbiggin take advantage of this lower sprawl of Baugh Fell's western shoulder, which culminates in the fine river scenery where Clough meets Rawthey.

The dogs of Fellgate may 'encourage' a wide berth

The walk's intimate river scenery is equalled by the extensive views from the base of the fell, the Howgills majestic in their entirety, from Winder to Wandale Hill.

Notices at Dovecote Gill suggest the wooded gill and cave are out of bounds

Map labels: KIRKBY STEPHEN A683, Hebblethwaite Hall, H.H. Woods, farm road, Hebblethwaite Hall Gill, ④, Sarthwaite, ruin, Baugh Fell, ⑤, Ghylass, Kiln, slopes of, Fellgate, ③, Dowbiggin, Wilkinstile, Dowbiggin Lane, Dovecote Gill, old Kiln, ②, N, pond, River Clough

WALK 8

BOWDERDALE AND HAZELGILL KNOTT

8¼ miles

from Bowderdale Foot

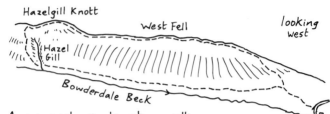

Hazelgill Knott

West Fell

looking west

Hazel Gill

Bowderdale Beck

Bowderdale Foot

A supremely simple return walk -
the deep confines of Bowderdale
contrast with the wide panoramas of
its enclosing ridge. Both share long miles!

Bowderdale is signposted off the A685. Park on the roadside
just before it drops down to the beck and the buildings.

THE WALK

Cross the bridge over Bowderdale Beck and up the
hill past the houses, and before a cattle-grid on the brow
leave the road by a wallside track on the left. This same
track runs through two enclosures before climbing to a gate
onto the open fell, at the very foot of the Hazelgill Knott
- West Fell ridge. Running left with the wall, the way forks
when the wall drops to the beck. This is the point to which
we shall return, but for now ignore the tractor track going
up the ridge, and opt for the path slanting down to commence
a long, long walk up Bowderdale.

Always keeping its distance above the beck, the path
forges on through the wilderness of this seemingly endless
dale, and only about 2½ miles since the fork does the time
come to turn up the steep flank for the ridge-top. This
crucial point occurs after crossing an inflowing beck (Hazel
Gill - note the lone tree part-way up) just yards beyond
Bowderdale Beck's major confluence with a beck of similar
proportions opposite. Leave the path for the grassy shoulder,
a direct climb that is really less of a pull than it might
appear - the going is aided by the terrace-like nature
of the grass. As steepness relents keep on across the
broad ridge to intercept the clear track along its crest.

Turning right for home, first task is the brief pull

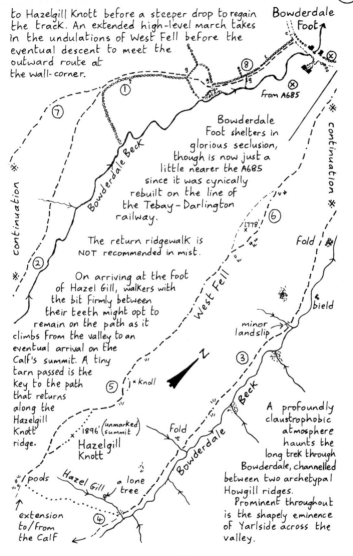

to Hazelgill Knott before a steeper drop to regain the track. An extended high-level march takes in the undulations of West Fell before the eventual descent to meet the outward route at the wall-corner.

Bowderdale Foot ↑

from A685 ⊗

Bowderdale Foot shelters in glorious seclusion, though is now just a little nearer the A685 since it was cynically rebuilt on the line of the Tebay–Darlington railway.

The return ridgewalk is NOT recommended in mist.

On arriving at the foot of Hazel Gill, walkers with the bit firmly between their teeth might opt to remain on the path as it climbs from the valley to an eventual arrival on the Calf's summit. A tiny tarn passed is the key to the path that returns along the Hazelgill Knott ridge.

continuation ✳

continuation ✳

continuation ✳

Bowderdale Beck

West Fell

1778'

Fold

bield

minor landslip

⑥

⑤ ⏐× knoll

×1896' (unmarked) (summit)
Hazelgill Knott

Fold

Bowderdale Beck

pods   Hazel Gill   a lone tree

extension to/from the Calf ← ④

A profoundly claustrophobic atmosphere haunts the long trek through Bowderdale, channelled between two archetypal Howgill ridges.

Prominent throughout is the shapely eminence of Yarlside across the valley.

WALK 9

7½ miles

| FOX'S PULPIT AND THE LUNE |

from Lowgill

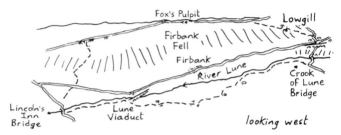

looking west

Firbank Fell offers glorious panoramas of the Howgills, while the return leg shadows the Lune along their base

Start from the staggered crossroads just above the defunct viaduct. Parking spaces on the roadside (B6257), 1½ miles south of A685 junction. This corner is also known as Beck Foot.

| THE WALK |

Leave the staggered crossroads by the minor road rising up past the phone box, leaving it almost at once by a short drive to a house on the left. An enclosed way rises up past the front of the house, and at a sharp bend where waymarks entice the Dales Way straight ahead, keep faith with the hedge to follow this sunken way left up to High House. Turn left down through the farmyard, passing between the farthest buildings to a rough lane rising away.

At the top keep straight on up the pathless field, following the left-hand wall over two stiles and then down to cross a marshy little stream. At the very point where stream and wall meet, a stile conveys you to the other side to follow another sunken way up to the Firbank Fell road. Turn briefly uphill for an undulating stride along its near traffic-free course to arrive at Fox's Pulpit.

On resuming the walk, the road declines gradually to pass a house on the left, and at the next cluster (New Field) turn left along a rough lane. At its early demise slant half-right across to a gate, then straight down the field-sides to enter a larger, sloping pasture. Just below a wall-corner on the left is a short row of trees, which can be followed down to a stile into Hawkrigg Wood. A lovely path slants down this all-too-short woodland interlude. On emerging maintain the slant left to a field-corner, below which is a gate onto the B6257. Cross straight over and on a short-lived path over the brow to drop down to the farm at Lincoln's Inn Bridge.

Cross the bridge with a wary eye on the traffic, and from a gate on the left commence the return to Crook of Lune Bridge and Lowgill. Along the riverbank the Lune Viaduct soon looms ahead, and the way passes under its tall arches before rising up the field. The path swings right then fades before crossing to a stile, from where a track heads away, with a parallel beck, to Low Branthwaite. Cross the farm road to a stile opposite, and follow the left-hand fence away. Rising up the field we become briefly enclosed: on emerging, cross to a gap-stile to the left of Bramaskew Farm, straight ahead. Continue on to another stile, and down a large field to a small barn. A track commences, becoming enclosed to lead to Nether Bainbridge.

Without entering its confines take a stile on the left, passing the rear of a barn then going left with the facing wall. Use a gate at a bend to climb to a little brow, then on to descend to Hole House Farm. Entering its yard, bear left along the private-looking way between dwellinghouses to a gate. A footbridge crosses Smithy Beck and the lower path leads down to a stile. Now cross to accompany the Lune through a large pasture below Thwaite Farm.

Another footbridge is crossed and the river remains in close company as far as a gate below Crook of Lune Farm up to the right. Follow the track away to join a narrow road descending to Crook of Lune Bridge, across which a short, steep climb concludes the walk by passing beneath the arches of Lowgill Viaduct.

The tablet on Firbank Fell

LET YOUR LIVES SPEAK

HERE OR NEAR THIS ROCK GEORGE FOX PREACHED TO ABOUT ONE THOUSAND SEEKERS FOR THREE HOURS ON SUNDAY JUNE 13, 1652. GREAT POWER INSPIRED HIS MESSAGE AND THE MEETING PROVED OF FIRST IMPORTANCE IN GATHERING THE SOCIETY OF FRIENDS KNOWN AS QUAKERS. MANY MEN AND WOMEN CONVINCED OF THE TRUTH ON THIS FELL AND IN OTHER PARTS OF THE NORTHERN COUNTIES WENT FORTH THROUGH THE LAND AND OVER THE SEAS WITH THE LIVING WORD OF THE LORD ENDURING GREAT HARDSHIPS AND WINNING MULTITUDES TO CHRIST.
JUNE 1952

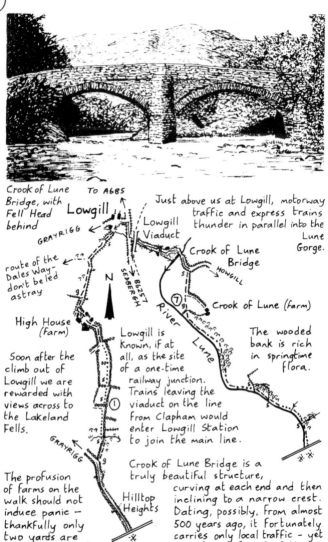

Crook of Lune Bridge, with Fell Head behind

TO A685

Lowgill

GRAYRIGG

Lowgill Viaduct

Just above us at Lowgill, motorway traffic and express trains thunder in parallel into the Lune Gorge.

Crook of Lune Bridge

HOWGILL

route of the Dales Way — don't be led astray

B6257 SEDBERGH

N

Crook of Lune (farm)

⑦

High House (farm)

River Lune

The wooded bank is rich in springtime flora.

Soon after the climb out of Lowgill we are rewarded with views across to the Lakeland Fells.

Lowgill is known, if at all, as the site of a one-time railway junction. Trains leaving the viaduct on the line from Clapham would enter Lowgill Station to join the main line.

①

GRAYRIGG

The profusion of farms on the walk should not induce panic — thankfully only two yards are actually entered.

Hilltop Heights

Crook of Lune Bridge is a truly beautiful structure, curving at each end and then inclining to a narrow crest. Dating, possibly, from almost 500 years ago, it fortunately carries only local traffic — yet is within half a mile of the M6.

Unassuming Firbank Fell is a place of pilgrimage by virtue of the windswept corner known as Fox's Pulpit. Here, in 1652, and fresh from his vision on Pendle Hill, George Fox addressed a multitude and thus began the Quaker movement. Adjacent to a memorial tablet is a tiny graveyard where a church once stood. This is an evocative spot that will cause many to lift their eyes heavenwards.

On the approach to Chapel Beck we encounter the river at close quarters, with a wide, stony bank leading the eye to Fell Head, in the Howgills.

The western Howgills dominate this walk, most impressively so during the march along the fell road. The Calf, as ever, sits back unobtrusively from its Kin.

Chapel Beck

Thwaite (Farm)

Smithy Beck

Hole House (Farm)

viewpoint on brow

450'

Nether Bainbridge (Farm)

River Lune

Bramaskew (Farm)

N

② Fox's Pulpit

Firbank Fell

From the vicinity of Bramaskew the church at Firbank is easily located, directly below our route over the fell. Also prominent on several occasions is the grassy line of the old railway across the Lune.

The fell road has views down the Lune Valley as far as the Bowland moors.

New Field

SEDBERGH

Low Branthwaite (Farm)

Lune Viaduct
Ford

Crosdale Beck

Map extended to show alternative path to Low Branthwaite if ford impassable.

The red sandstone and metal arches of the Lune Viaduct appear in dramatic fashion above a pastoral scene.

③

Hawkrigg Wood

B6257

ROAD

④

Lincoln's Inn Bridge

SEDBERGH A684

On emerging, shapely Winder appears across the Lune

KENDAL A684

the farm is, not surprisingly, a former hostelry.

Lune Viaduct

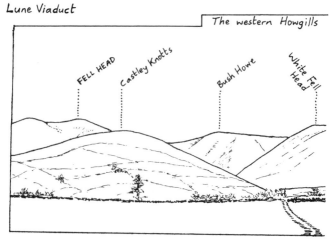

The western Howgills

FELL HEAD

Castley Knotts

Bush Howe

White Fell Head

Lincoln's Inn Bridge
and the Lune

From above Hole House

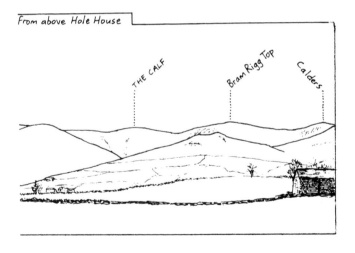

THE CALF

Bram Rigg Top

Calders

WALK 10

5¾ miles

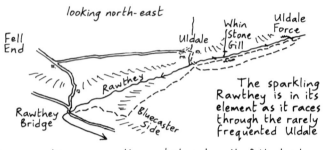

| THE ULDALE WATERFALLS |

from Rawthey Bridge

looking north-east

The sparkling
Rawthey is in its
element as it races
through the rarely
frequented Uldale

Large parking area on the roadside just south of the bridge

| THE WALK |

By the roadside National Park boundary sign, a gate sees a track set off into an uninspiring marshy tract. It quickly escapes to climb a grooved route to the right. At the brow it fords a marshy beck, and here leave the old green road by a sharp left branch bound for a level march into Uldale. The track is clear throughout as it runs along to arrive above a footbridge below the inflowing Needlehouse Gill, a bridge to which we shall return after visiting the waterfalls.

Already the first falls are in view, and a thin path shadows the Rawthey to approach them and then climb past. Easy going on a sometimes sketchy path leads to a short, bouldery section below the wall of Rawthey Gill Quarry. Towards the end the splendid fall of Whin Stone Gill calls for a halt, while just beyond, a slight rise brings the walk's highlight, Uldale Force into distant view. En route, however, a more modest waterfall intervenes, and this unexpected near-impasse necessitates a clamber up the steep slope, traversing cautiously above a sheer drop to progress further.

If satisfied with the view of Uldale Force from this point, then take advantage of height gained to rise again to locate a slim trod above the ravine. Otherwise drop back towards the beck to forge on the final 200 yards – again with care near the end - to stand in the profound amphitheatre at the very foot of the tumbling waters.

Here, at Uldale Force, the path most emphatically terminates. Onward progress thus barred, retrace steps only a few yards to scamper up the grassy bank to low outcrops lining the top. The aforementioned slender trod is gained and facilitates an excellent return walk high along the edge of the gill's confines, offering a thorough overview which includes fresh sightings of Whin Stone Gill Falls and retrospects of Uldale Force. Little more than a sheeptrod, our way runs along to a fold, appropriately enough, then quickly peters out. By now it is about time to work a way steadily down to return to the footbridge.

An enclosed track mounts the opposite flank, rising through woodland to meet the road to Uldale House. Turn left along it to merge with one from Needle House, thence running out across the moor to a T-junction at Fell End. Turn left along the equally quiet old road of the 'street', to soon drop tidily down to Rawthey Bridge.

Uldale
Force

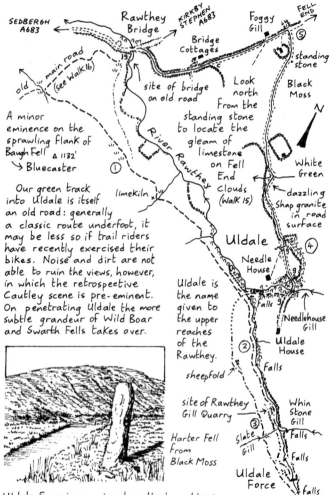

Rawthey Bridge

KIRKBY STEPHEN A683

Foggy Gill

FELL END

SEDBERGH A683

Bridge Cottages

⑤

standing stone

old main road (see Walk 16)

old

site of bridge on old road

Look north from the standing stone to locate the gleam of limestone on Fell End Clouds (Walk 15)

Black Moss

White Green

A minor eminence on the sprawling flank of Baugh Fell △1132'
→ Bluecaster

River Rawthey

①

limekiln

dazzling Shap granite in road surface

Our green track into Uldale is itself an old road: generally a classic route underfoot, it may be less so if trail riders have recently exercised their bikes. Noise and dirt are not able to ruin the views, however, in which the retrospective Cautley scene is pre-eminent. On penetrating Uldale the more subtle grandeur of Wild Boar and Swarth Fells takes over.

Uldale

Needle House

④

Uldale is the name given to the upper reaches of the Rawthey.

Needlehouse Gill

Uldale House

falls

②

sheepfold

site of Rawthey Gill Quarry

③

Whin Stone Gill

Slate Gill

Falls

falls

Harter Fell from Black Moss

Uldale Force

falls

Uldale Force is a major drop, Hardraw-like in its setting, but if anything a better fall of water. Here one pays in effort, rather than shillings, for the pleasure. Just above, and worth a visit, is a contrastingly delicate, open-air little fall.

WALK 11

6 miles

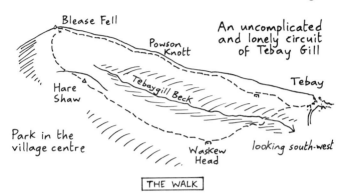

| BLEASE FELL AND TEBAY GILL |

from Tebay

An uncomplicated
and lonely circuit
of Tebay Gill

Park in the
village centre

looking south-west

| THE WALK |

Leave Mount Pleasant at the top of the village by an unassuming road rising past the old school, now operating as a youth hostel. It crosses a cattle-grid onto the open moor, and rises away to serve several farms. On the brow near a wall-corner it loses its full surface, and here take a second track branching right to rise alongside the wall.

The track runs past the farm buildings of Tebaygill, and as it starts to drop towards the beck, leave it by a fork onto the grassy ridge. From here on a generally clear track scales the fell at the most generous of gradients, over the brow of Powson Knott and a further knoll to gain the peaty summit of Blease Fell. Full compensation for the absence of a cairn in this bleak spot is found in the neat structure occupying a far worthier position a little beyond: this is the place to break the journey.

Doubling back to the left a marshy crossing to Hare Shaw is quickly accomplished, bearing a little right avoids the worst of the wet ground. From the cairn head north down the broad ridge, with a pleasant, grassy surface and an intermittent tractor track returning. The minor swelling of Knott can be topped or skirted to the left before more level terrain leads to the farm buildings of Waskew Head.

Its access track – with grassier alternatives – leads straight down to cross Tebaygill Beck and so meet up with the outward route for the final few minutes.

45

The valley of Carlin Gill from Blease Fell,
with Fell Head rising behind (scene of Walk 5).

Blease Fell's summit appears at
the pools, with Fell Head peeping
over the Hare Shaw col.

The buzz of the Lune Gorge
is immediately below
Blease Fell's flanks.

Hare Shaw is
prominent
throughout
the climb
to Blease
Fell.

Powson
Knott
1227' ×

The pull
to the knoll
of Powson Knott
might earn a halt
to savour the
Lakeland
skyline
beyond the
lovely environs of Borrowdale,
ranging from the Coniston
group to the High
Street range.

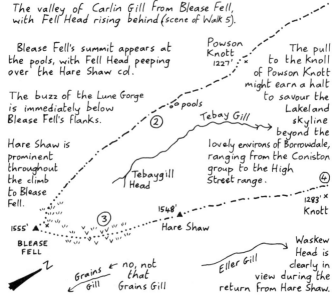

pools

② Tebay Gill

Tebaygill
Head

1555' ▲ ×

BLEASE
FELL

③

1548'
Hare Shaw

④

1283' ×
Knott

Grains
Gill ← no, not
that
Grains Gill

Eller Gill

Waskew
Head is
clearly in
view during the
return from Hare Shaw.

Tebay is an unassuming village, for decades known only as a name on the railway map of Britain. That distinction has been lost, and replaced, for better or for worse, by the constant drone of the M6 motorway and its attendant access. Detached from the village – as is the hamlet of Old Tebay – are rows of railway cottages, overlooking the junction of the dismantled branch to Darlington with the main line (west) to Scotland. They don't stop here anymore though...

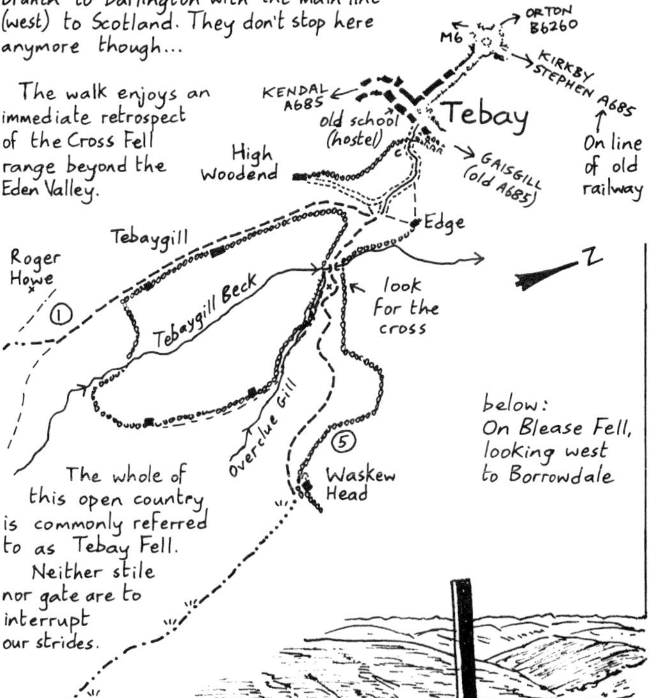

The walk enjoys an immediate retrospect of the Cross Fell range beyond the Eden Valley.

ORTON B6260

M6

KIRKBY STEPHEN A685

KENDAL A685

old school (hostel)

Tebay

GAISGILL (old A685)

On line of old railway

High Woodend

Tebaygill

Roger Howe

①

Tebaygill Beck

Edge

look for the cross

N

Overclue Gill

⑤

Waskew Head

The whole of this open country is commonly referred to as Tebay Fell.

Neither stile nor gate are to interrupt our strides.

below:
On Blease Fell, looking west to Borrowdale

WALK 12

12½ miles

THE MIDDLETON FELL CIRCUIT

from Barbon

Barkin Top   Calf Top   Castle Knott

Middleton Fell

Fellside

Eskholme Pike △

Middleton Hall

Middleton

looking east   A683   Barbon

An emphatic leg-stretcher
encircling the wide skyline
of this unsung mountain

Park in the village centre

THE WALK

Leave the village by the road past the church, then turning along the drive into Barbon Park. Across the bridge the drive swings right to climb to Barbon Manor, but here keep straight on over the grass to pass outside the top end of a small wood. From the gate at the end keep on to the buildings at Eskholme, there following a crumbling wall up to the right. The gate at the top is the last for a good few miles, and the ascent can begin in earnest with a steep pull up short-cropped grass to the cairn on Eskholme Pike. Features on the way include a natural stone chair, the slab of Devil's Crag, and a stone-built shelter.

Behind the cairn a thin trod makes for the nearby wall, but a better one sets an obvious course on the crest of the grassy ridge: visible ahead is the cairn atop Castle Knott, some way off and still some way short of the main summit. For now the gentle slope eases further and the path fades for a time before returning to wind up and run on between a tidy cairn and a clutch of tiny pools. Up above, the top of Castle Knott beckons.

On gaining Castle Knott's cairn, a surprise is in store in the form of a substantial depression interrupting the march to Calf Top. At least the summit of the fell is visible now, and the high ridge is quickly attained on a sometimes sketchy path. A delightful pull through the heather precedes a simple stroll to the Ordnance column.

Descent is hardly the right word to describe the rambling miles ahead, the only task being to remain on the broad ridge-top for a good couple of miles, in the constant company of either the wall or a replacement fence that were first encountered just prior to the Felltop. A good track is underfoot the entire way, some heathery sections rising still further above the general loveliness.

After a near-level stretch, a tiny stone shelter is the indicator that our track is to finally leave the endless ridge - and its endless wall - for the Lune Valley. After a good deal of meandering the farm at Fellside appears below, and the luxuriant green way grudgingly vacates the fell. Passing between the buildings, the farm road takes over to wind down to the main road, though just past a fence a broad green way cuts a corner on the left to emerge rather tidily alongside the aptly-named hostelry.

Without the luxury of a waiting chauffeur, the road walk begins: be sure to turn left! Happily the main road is quickly departed at a junction beyond a railway bridge. At this very point one can appraise Middleton Hall just up a farm road before setting forth along the back road-known as High Lane - for eventual return to Barbon. Varying degrees of narrowness are exhibited by this lane serving a string of farms along the base of Middleton Fell, and before too long hopefully, it will emerge into the centre of Barbon.

Devil's Crag, Eskholme Pike

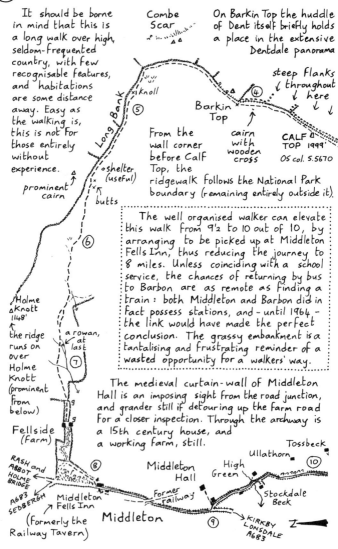

It should be borne in mind that this is a long walk over high, seldom-frequented country, with few recognisable features, and habitations are some distance away. Easy as the walking is, this is not for those entirely without experience.

prominent cairn

Combe Scar

On Barkin Top the huddle of Dent itself briefly holds a place in the extensive Dentdale panorama

steep flanks throughout here

Long Bank

×knoll

⑤

Barkin Top

④

From the wall corner before Calf Top, the ridgewalk follows the National Park boundary (remaining entirely outside it).

cairn with wooden cross

CALF TOP 1999' OS col. 5.5670

o shelter (useful)

butts

⑥

The well organised walker can elevate this walk from 9½ to 10 out of 10, by arranging to be picked up at Middleton Fells Inn, thus reducing the journey to 8 miles. Unless coinciding with a school service, the chances of returning by bus to Barbon are as remote as finding a train: both Middleton and Barbon did in fact possess stations, and - until 1964 - the link would have made the perfect conclusion. The grassy embankment is a tantalising and frustrating reminder of a wasted opportunity for a walkers' way.

Holme Knott 1148'

the ridge runs on over Holme Knott (prominent from below)

a rowan, at last

⑦

The medieval curtain-wall of Middleton Hall is an imposing sight from the road junction, and grander still if detouring up the farm road for a closer inspection. Through the archway is a 15th century house, and a working farm, still.

Tossbeck

Ullathorn

Fellside (Farm)

⑧

Middleton Hall

High Green

⑩

Stockdale Beck

RASH and ABBOT HOLME BRIDGE

A683 SEDBERGH

Middleton Fells Inn

Former railway

KIRKBY LONSDALE A683

Middleton

⑨

(formerly the Railway Tavern)

Middleton Fell - or Fells - as the mass is sometimes known - is very much a detached parcel of upland, largely outwith the Dales National Park as a result of its allegiance to Westmorland. Few walkers venture here, thanks in part to its lack of (literally) inches. It is certainly most at home in the Howgills area however, For its characteristics are Howgill-like in its occasional slaty outcrops.

Perhaps its best comparison is with Black Combe in the south Lakes, For its slatiness is matched by its deeply incised western gills, its heather flanks, its isolation, and even its 'limitations' of altitude.

Calf Top, its summit, grants extensive views over the north-west counties: a hurdle in the fence gives access to a contrasting close-up view down its sheer east flank.

steep slopes here

③

Castle Knott

Fold

pools

②

Southdale Beck

The environs of Castle Knott offer dramatic views over Barbondale to Crag Hill, on Great Coum.

Note that this map is at a scale smaller than the rest of the book

The return walk along the back road is largely cushioned between leafy hedgerows, and gives good glimpses into the hidden combes and - from here at least - shapely ridge-ends of Middleton Fell.

Barbon Manor (not seen) was built as a Victorian shooting lodge

Eskholme Pike

Barbon Manor

Barbon Beck

Devil's Crag ①

stone chair

Barbon Park

Eskholme

DENT

Eskholme Pike is highly prominent from below, and when attained it well merits a halt to survey a superb Lune Valley panorama. Devil's Crag is somewhat ambitiously named.

Barbon

Sowermires

Applegarth

Borwen

⑫

TO A683 KIRKBY LONSDALE

Millbeck ⑪

School House

Z

The attractive village of Barbon nestles in a fine Lune Valley setting at the foot of the Dales' westernmost fells. In spite of its enviable location it is a 'tourist-free' area. A narrow road squeezes through the hills to emerge into the heart of Dentdale. The pleasing church of St. Bartholomew is a mere century old.

51

WALK 13

5½ miles

ARANT HAW, WINDER AND CROOK

From Sedbergh

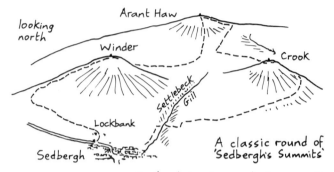

looking north

A classic round of 'Sedbergh's Summits'

Sedbergh has two central car parks

THE WALK

Leave the main street by Joss Lane rising past the car park. It swings up to the right. From its demise at a gate a farm road to Hill takes over, while our way slants to the top corner of the field. A path climbs with Settlebeck Gill to gain the open fell at a quaint old gate. With a choice of paths, take the less obvious one, running down to ford the beck above a waterfall.

The steep slope behind conceals a sunken track up to the corner of the intake wall. Now locate the good pathway sloping to the right, through bracken across the face of Crook. It is impeccably graded throughout, and soon after swinging left above Ashbeck Gill, a fork is reached: take the sunken way climbing left, and as it peters out the cairn atop Crook will be quickly gained, up to the left.

Both Winder and Arant Haw can now be appraised, and the way to the latter is a largely pathless march, initially, keeping to the height of land to intercept the main path on the entire Howgills above the beginnings of Settlebeck Gill. This popular thoroughfare links Sedbergh with the Calf, and its green carpet transports us across Arant Haw's upper slopes to a distinct brow, where the main path falls to a depression before climbing to Calders and thence the Calf: our way, however, doubles back up to the left on a

vague trod rising effortlessy to the summit of Arant Haw.
Leave the scrappy cairn for the Sedbergh (southern) edge of the broad top, where a clear path is found to make a no-nonsense descent to the Sedbergh-Calf path. Bearing right at two successive junctions the ascent of the day's third summit is rapidly accomplished, the way having been entirely apparent since departing Arant Haw. Winder's cairn and Ordnance column are now vacated by a path striking west towards the Lune, an outstanding green way that descends to within yards of the intake wall. Turn left to find a narrow path through bracken, meeting up with the wall as Sedbergh appears ahead. At a gate drop down through Lockbank Farm onto Howgill Lane, turning left to finish.

Above: Arant Haw and Winder from the south-west

Below: The summit
of Crook

Arant Haw, Winder and Crook are the southernmost tops of the Howgills, each exhibiting characteristics to be found throughout the group. Together they form a splendid introduction to the Howgill Fells. The paths linking them together are a great joy to tread, the backbone of the walk being the main path in the whole group, and from which all three tops are accessible.

Crook's top offers sweeping early views over Garsdale and the valley of the Rawthey backed by Baugh Fell, while its summit cairn brings an early sighting of the Lakeland Fells.

Arant Haw, as the parent fell, offers most extensive views, though its finest prospect is that of the high Howgills immediately to the north.

Winder retains the open vistas, added to which it enjoys a more intimate picture of Sedbergh, backed by Dentdale stretching into the haze. This is entirely fitting, as Winder is popularly regarded as the town's own 'special' fell.

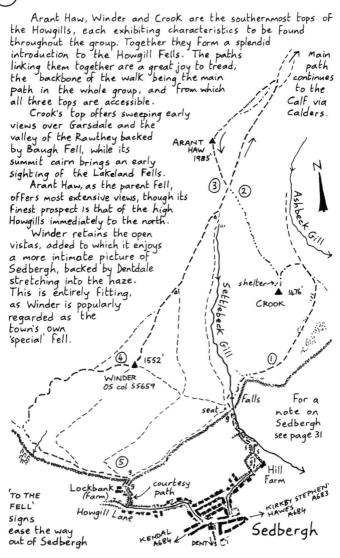

Main path continues to the Calf via Calders.

ARANT HAW 1985

N

Ashbeck Grill

③ ②

Settlebeck Gill

shelter→ 1476' CROOK

①

④ 1552'
WINDER
OS col. 55659

falls

seat

⑤

For a note on Sedbergh see page 31

g

g
Lockbank (Farm)

courtesy path

Howgill Lane

Hill Farm

KIRKBY STEPHEN A683

HAWES A684

KENDAL A684

DENT ¾

Sedbergh

'TO THE FELL' signs ease the way out of Sedbergh

54

WALK 14

6¼ miles

LOWER GARSDALE

from Garsdale Foot

A modest stroll through the fields and an impressive length of riverbank in the shadow of giant fells

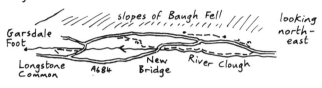

Start from the large parking area on Longstone Common, 2½ miles out of Sedbergh where the Hawes road becomes unfenced

THE WALK

Leave the car park by the minor road dropping to cross the river Clough at Danny Bridge, and follow this traffic-free byway updale for a good mile and a half. Several farms are passed and several gates are met. Eventually, after a short, steep pull just beyond a farm on a sharp bend, take a gate on the left labelled *Bellow Hill*. Follow the drive to the first wall, then branch right to a stile. Continue away with the wall to cross a tiny beck, and on again to a stile before aiming for the farm of Pike Hill ahead. A stile gives access to its lane which can be followed down to the road.

Go left for a quarter-mile or so, taking greater care as this is now the main road, not the back lane, and its verges offer little refuge. At the allotted distance — just beyond the first farm on the right - locate a half-hidden stile on the left at a bend. Follow the wall away, crossing a drive and on through a second field to find the next stile just left of a barn. From a tiny beck rise over the field to a gate, then across to a stile back onto the road. Head left once again, the road thankfully being far more accommodating this time. As it swings down to the river, take up the offer of a stile just beyond a barn.

In the company of the Clough the return leg now begins. At the end of the first pasture some trees briefly keep the river at bay, but otherwise a long and

55

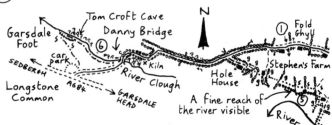

pleasant walk clings to the wooded bank all
the way to New Bridge. While the main road
crosses the river, the walk merely crosses the road
to descend some steps in order to continue downstream.

At the first field boundary however, it is time to
leave the Clough and head up the field-side towards a
barn. Go through a hand-gate just before it, and up the
small enclosure to a gate on the left of the barn. Slant
half-left up to a stile, then running along through several
fields to arrive at the front of Stephen's Farm. Continue
across until Hole House Farm appears, and from a gate at the
right side of a tiny plantation its yard will be entered.

The farm drive heads away to rejoin the outward
lane, to now return to Danny Bridge. On crossing it, a fine
conclusion can be incorporated by following the geological
trail downstream. It ends beyond a short fenced section, and
an initially sketchy path slants back up to the car park.

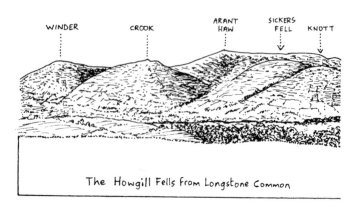

The Howgill Fells from Longstone Common

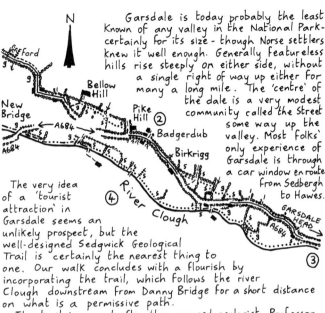

Garsdale is today probably the least known of any valley in the National Park - certainly for its size - though Norse settlers knew it well enough. Generally featureless hills rise steeply on either side, without a single right of way up either for many a long mile. The 'centre' of the dale is a very modest community called the Street some way up the valley. Most folks' only experience of Garsdale is through a car window en route from Sedbergh to Hawes.

The very idea of a 'tourist attraction' in Garsdale seems an unlikely prospect, but the well-designed Sedgwick Geological Trail is certainly the nearest thing to one. Our walk concludes with a flourish by incorporating the trail, which follows the river Clough downstream from Danny Bridge for a short distance on what is a permissive path.

The trail is named after the renowned geologist Professor Adam Sedgwick, born in neighbouring Dentdale in 1785 and 50 years at Cambridge: in recognition of his research locally, a detailed leaflet (available in Sedbergh or at the car park) tells what to look for in this remarkable area of the important Dent Fault.

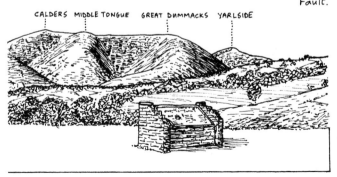

CALDERS   MIDDLE TONGUE   GREAT DUMMACKS   YARLSIDE

WALK 15

STENNERSKEUGH AND FELL END CLOUDS

3¾ miles

from The Street

looking south-east

An absorbing
stroll through unfrequented
limestone country that ranks with the finest

Start from the old quarry on the old road (The Street) just
as it leaves the A683 near Stennerskeugh (signposted Uldale and
Fell End). Grid reference: 734005

THE WALK

From the quarry turn right (north) along the Street
to join the main road, which is followed right for a minute
only before branching right on a grassy wallside track. It runs
along the front of the Street Farm, and continuing on it
becomes enclosed to pass between the buildings at the
Street. Keep straight on (right) on the surfaced road to
Stennerskeugh, and at the first opportunity double back
up to the right on the walled track known as Clouds Lane.
At a gate it gains the open fell, on which a right-
hand track is most suitable, rising by the wall which soon
swings right. Keeping above the wall, a pathless amble
now ensues along a grassy shelf sandwiched between tiers
of limestone: these are Stennerskeugh Clouds. Continue on
until the pronounced hollow of Dale Slack, and here turn
left up a green track taking advantage of the breach.
Straight ahead are Fell End Clouds, and when the
track fades atop the outcrops turn right, again picking
your own route influenced by the natural line of the scars.
Numerous cairns loiter about the limestone pavements, and
at the far end a single, substantial cairn precedes a lone
tree by some old workings. These mark the terminus of the
clouds, so bear down to the right to pick up a thin track
running down past two limekilns onto the Street. Turn
right on its accommodating verge to return to the quarry.

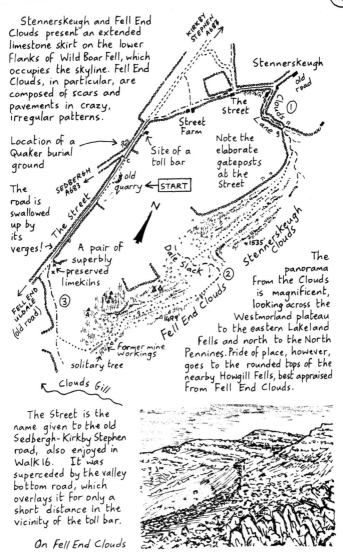

Stennerskeugh and Fell End Clouds present an extended limestone skirt on the lower flanks of Wild Boar Fell, which occupies the skyline. Fell End Clouds, in particular, are composed of scars and pavements in crazy, irregular patterns.

KIRKBY STEPHEN A683

Stennerskeugh

old road

Clouds ① Lane

The Street

Street Farm

Location of a Quaker burial ground →

Note the elaborate gateposts at the Street

SEDBERGH A683

The Street

Site of a toll bar

old quarry START

The road is swallowed up by its verges! →

The Street

N

A pair of superbly preserved limekilns

FELL END ULDALE (old road)

③

Dale Slack

*1535'

Stennerskeugh Clouds

②

Fell End Clouds

Former mine workings

solitary tree

Clouds Gill

The panorama from the Clouds is magnificent, looking across the Westmorland plateau to the eastern Lakeland Fells and north to the North Pennines. Pride of place, however, goes to the rounded tops of the nearby Howgill Fells, best appraised from Fell End Clouds.

The Street is the name given to the old Sedbergh-Kirkby Stephen road, also enjoyed in Walk 16. It was superceded by the valley bottom road, which overlays it for only a short distance in the vicinity of the toll bar.

On Fell End Clouds

WALK 16

CAUTLEY SPOUT AND THE RAWTHEY

6¼ miles

from Cautley

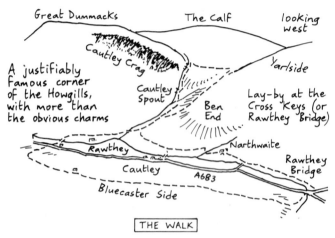

Great Dummacks — The Calf — looking west

Cautley Crag

A justifiably famous corner of the Howgills, with more than the obvious charms

Cautley Spout

Ben End

Yarlside

Lay-by at the Cross Keys (or Rawthey Bridge)

Rawthey

Cautley

Narthwaite

Rawthey Bridge

A683

Bluecaster Side

THE WALK

Cross the footbridge over the Rawthey just above the inn, and go straight ahead onto a wide track. Turn right along it, continuing as a pleasant green path to ford Backside Beck (a challenge after a wet spell) before a short pull to Narthwaite. Leave the farm buildings by the drive on the right, following it almost all the way down to the main road. A gate on a sharp bend points the way along a lesser track which ends at a wood. Through a gate, ford a stream to follow a path along the wood-bottom, and when the fence turns right it slants down to follow the Rawthey upstream. Emerging from the trees to cross a brace of fields, a tiny stream is crossed (by a bridge, at last!) to rise onto the road just above Rawthey Bridge.

Within a few yards of crossing the bridge take a gate on the left, from where a track heading away almost at once turns sketchily right in a distinctly 'moist' neighbourhood. Soon the track improves, and after a gentle rise it starts to run parallel with but high above the main road. Shortly after going past Bluecaster Cottage a gate is reached at a lane-head, and just after it take a gate on the right to descend a sunken track onto the road.

Cross the main road and down a farm road over the Rawthey and through the fields to Cautley Thwaite Farm. Keep straight on through two gates and to the right of a barn, then going a little left to a gate to emerge on a good path. Soon Cautley Holme Beck is crossed by a basic bridge, from where a path runs along to the foot of Cautley Spout. To enjoy a closer look, cross the side beck and tackle the steep path by the gill. Caution is urged when peering into the lower fall, which is partially obscured by hardy foliage.

Continuing up, the upper falls are free of obstruction and can be savoured more leisurely. At the top the path levels out, and here leave it after locating a trod along to the right. After a steady traverse it fades, leaving you to slant down to the incisive pass of Bowderdale Head. Turning right a good path forms to return with the side beck to the foot of the Spout. Omitting Cautley Holme Beck, head back round the base of Yarlside on the 'tourist' path, turning upstream with the Rawthey to quickly return to the footbridge at the start.

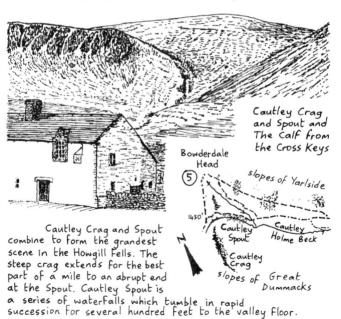

Cautley Crag and Spout and The Calf from the Cross Keys

Bowderdale Head

5

1450'

slopes of Yarlside

Cautley Spout

Cautley Holme Beck

Cautley Crag

N

slopes of Great Dummacks

Cautley Crag and Spout combine to form the grandest scene in the Howgill Fells. The steep crag extends for the best part of a mile to an abrupt end at the Spout. Cautley Spout is a series of waterfalls which tumble in rapid succession for several hundred feet to the valley floor.

The river Rawthey flows for sixteen miles from near the lonely summit of Baugh Fell to its acceptance into the Lune beyond Sedbergh. On the journey there it absorbs the waters of the Clough and the Dee. All is preciously unspoilt hereabouts, and in the neighbourhood of this walk the river exudes all its charms, flowing along a green valley bottom with bare fells rising on each side.

Rawthey Bridge marks the old Yorkshire-Westmorland boundary and, as a result, the illogical National Park boundary also. Between the prosaicly titled Backside Beck and the bridge we therefore tread a mile of old Westmorland.

The Cross Keys is that rare creature the temperance inn. Though labelled Cautley there is no definable centre, just a scattering of farms, dwellings and a church along the Sedbergh road.

The farm bridge over the Rawthey at Wardses is surprisingly high: note the intense clarity of the water.

Semi-wild ponies graze this open fell.

From Rawthey Bridge to beyond Bluecaster we tread the old road to Kirkby Stephen, once the main highway through these hills. Constructed well above the valley floor, it now forms a green promenade with truly outstanding views across to the eastern Howgills. (see also Walk 10)

Map labels: KIRKBY STEPHEN A683 · Rawthey Bridge · ULDALE · Murthwaite Park · A683 · ① · Handley's Bridge · ② · Ⓝ · slopes of Wandale Hill · Narthwaite (Farm) · River Rawthey · ford · Backside Beck · old fold · A683 · Bluecaster Side · slopes of Yarlside · Cross Keys Cautley · A683 · ⑥ · ford · Low Haygarth (Farm) · Bluecaster Cottage · ③ · Cautley Holme Beck · ④ · slopes of Great Dummacks · Cautley Thwaite (Farm) · Wardses (Farm) · ↓ SEDBERGH A683

LOG OF THE WALKS

These two pages provide an opportunity to maintain a permanent record of the walks completed

WALK	DATE	TIME Start	TIME Finish	WEATHER	COMMENTS
1					
2					
3					
4					
5					
6					
7					
8					

LOG OF THE WALKS continued

WALK	DATE	TIME Start	Finish	WEATHER	COMMENTS
9					
10					
11					
12					
13					
14					
15					
16					